MW00782180

Remember the 15 points:

1. Don't be a hero . . . accept your situation and be prepared to wait.
2. The first 15 to 45 minutes are the most dangerous. Follow instructions.
3. Don't speak unless spoken to, and then only when necessary.
4. Try to rest.
5. Don't make suggestions.
6. Escape? Should you or shouldn't you? THINK TWICE!
7. Advise on and request medication or aid if needed.
8. Be observant. You may be released and can help the authorities.
9. Be prepared to talk to the police on the telephone.
10. Don't be argumentative.
11. Treat the captor like royalty.
12. Be patient.
13. A black or red passport (diplomatic and official, respectively) may not bring you the best of privileges.
14. Get rid of items that could single you out as a person your captors might be fearful of.
15. If rescue comes, be prepared to HIT THE DECK.

How to Be a Hostage and Live

🔳🔳🔳🔳🔳🔳🔳🔳🔳🔳🔳🔳🔳🔳🔳🔳🔳🔳🔳🔳🔳🔳🔳🔳🔳🔳🔳🔳🔳🔳🔳

by FRANK A. BOLZ, JR.

Lyle Stuart Inc.   Secaucus, New Jersey

Copyright © 1987 by Frank A. Bolz, Jr.

Published by Lyle Stuart Inc.
120 Enterprise Ave., Secaucus, N.J. 07094
In Canada: Musson Book Company
a division of General Publishing Co. Limited
Don Mills, Ontario

All rights reserved. No part of this book
may be reproduced in any form, except by
a newspaper or magazine reviewer who wishes
to quote brief passages in connection
with a review.

Queries regarding rights and permissions should be
addressed to: Lyle Stuart, 120 Enterprise Avenue
Secaucus, N.J. 07094

Manufactured in the United States of America

ISBN 0-8184-0426-4

*Dedicated to all those who have been
held hostage, and to their families*

Contents

How to Protect Yourself If Held Hostage

You are a hostage. It could happen on an airplane, train, boat or bus. Day-to-day activities in stores, supermarkets, banks, airports as well as bars, restaurants, churches and prisons can be the scene. Anywhere people pass, congregate or conduct business can be the stage for a hostage drama, and you can be one of the players.

Though there is no guarantee that if you follow these

suggestions it won't happen to you, or that all will turn out fine, you will definitely reduce the risk, probability and the inherent dangers of being held hostage.

The points that will be covered are gained from almost 14 years of "hands on" experience in hostage negotiation and recovery. Frank Bolz has personally handled more than 285 hostage and hijacking incidents, bringing about the release of more than 850 hostages without the loss of a life.

The author has interviewed and debriefed numerous persons who were either held hostage or were kidnapped, and has gleaned many of the fine points from these discourses. This information and knowledge will assist you should the inauspicious event take place.

The following points underscore some of the "Do's" and "Don'ts" if actually taken hostage. They range from stationary incidents such as occur in homes and businesses, to mobile hijackings on aircraft, vehicles or ships. All these examples will be amplified in this book.

Remember, it can happen to anyone . . . from delivery boy to the corporate manager, vacationer to seasoned traveler, student to diplomat. No one is immune. Fate and circumstance merely set the stage, how you personally react greatly affects the outcome.

In the formulation of the N.Y.C. Police Department's Hostage Recovery Program, my colleague Detective Harvey Schlossberg, Phd., and I researched and postulated that there were certain psychological principles and dynamics that direct hostage incidents. One of these, and a very important one at that, is: "The hostage, in and of himself, has no value to the perpetrator other than for the audience that he can create."

When hostages are taken, they are used as leverage against the authorities. It may be as a "ticket to freedom" by a criminal in a scheme gone awry, or as a means to get a "manifesto" published for a political, revolutionary or terrorist organization. It may also be a means for a disgruntled employee or a distraught spouse to get attention for their real or imagined grievances.

We see this demonstrated constantly in international terrorist incidents that both grasp and then manipulate our media. They play the media back and forth, almost as an angler plays a game fish, holding taut then yielding, then taut again.

In order to help you remember some of the very important points of survival, they have been outlined in the following short phrases. These are amplified further in succeeding chapters.

1. Don't be a hero . . . accept your situation and be prepared to wait. Patience here is a *definite* virtue.
2. The first 15 to 45 minutes are the most dangerous. Everyone is in a state of panic. Follow instructions.
3. Don't speak unless spoken to, and then only when necessary.
4. Try to rest.
5. Don't make suggestions.
6. Escape? Should you or shouldn't you . . . THINK TWICE!

7. Advise on and request special medication or aid if needed.
8. Be observant. You may be released and can help the authorities.
9. Be prepared to talk to the police on the telephone.
10. Don't be argumentative.
11. Treat the captor like royalty.
12. Be patient.
13. A black or red passport (diplomatic and official, respectively) may not bring you the best of privileges.
14. Get rid of items that could single you out as a person your captors might be fearful of.
15. If rescue comes, be prepared to HIT THE DECK! Get down and follow any shouted commands quickly, keeping your hands on your head.

Don't Be a Hero. Accept Your Situation and Be Prepared to Wait

This point is very difficult for some people to accept. Often the subjects of a kidnapping or hijacking are business executives or ranking government officials. They did not attain their position in business or government by being docile or laid back. They are accustomed to issuing orders, not to carrying them out. The same applies to airline pilots and flight crews. They go from being master of the vessel and chief authority figures to being just another captive of the hijacker or hostage-taker.

One of the first things the perpetrators will try to do is

to break the spirit of their victims. They will try to reduce them to an almost infantile state where they must ask for permission for anything and everything, including eating, sleeping and even going to the toilet. In more than one kidnap incident, the first thing done to the victim was to strip him completely naked, placing him in an embarrassing and fearful state with only a slop-pot or hole in the corner for personal hygiene. Start by establishing a routine as quickly as possible. Make a quick assessment of your surroundings. One must make every effort to maintain his dignity without being arrogant or brazen. This will usually win the respect of the captors, but be careful not to make it a challenge.

The First 15 to 45 Minutes Are the Most Dangerous. Follow Instructions

When the initial incident takes place, the hostages are in the gravest danger. This is because the perpetrators are going through a panic reaction, a high anxiety situation which is manifested by the "fight or flight" mechanism. If the hostages hesitate or offer ANY overt resistance, the perpetrators will try to demonstrate that they have the power. In order for a small number of terrorists to control a large number of people the captors often engage in a quick violent act. They may beat someone, make a lot of noise or even kill someone indiscriminantly. If there is no resistance, just a lot of noise may be sufficient.

These first few minutes are the most dangerous for *all*

concerned. This includes the hostages, the responding or confronting authorities and even the perpetrator. In one instance, at Lod airport in Israel, in the frenzy of the takeover the terrorist accidentally shot one of his cohorts.

Once the perpetrator feels comparatively "safe" in his cocoon, he will start to relax. This sense of calm settling in will become apparent from the voices of the captors. Then, as we will discuss later, the stage is set for the "Stockholm syndrome" to develop.

Don't Speak Unless Spoken to, and Then Only When Necessary

If you create an atmosphere where you stand out, then you may be singled out by the perpetrator to demonstrate the seriousness of their threat. There have been incidents where individuals have been selected from the crowd of hostages, and were brought to the door of the aircraft or building to be publicly beaten or executed. Recently in Middle East hijackings, for instance (Kuwaiti Airline hijacking in December of 1984, and the TWA flight 847 hijacking of 1985), the mere fact that individuals were Americans or Israelis, or even had "Jewish sounding names" was sufficient reason for their captors to single them out.

When possible, try to make eye contact with the captors when they speak to you and when you respond. This has been proven difficult in some recent cases where the terrorists required everyone to sit with their heads down in the "crash position." This is often done so that a small number of persons can maintain control over a larger group of victims. Eye contact will assist in establishing rapport. (NOTE: Be careful not to stare at, or "look down" upon your captors. This might be considered threatening.)

Try to Rest

As absurd as this may sound to anyone "under the gun," it is a very important and useful guideline. The effects of panic after the initial seizure will wear both victims and captors down, psychologically and physiologically. With the constant raising and lowering of anxieties, all concerned can become exhausted. This may not pertain to the captors if they are "chemically supported," using drugs or other stimulants.

It is not surprising or uncommon for everyone to fall asleep, hostage and hostage-taker alike. This is especially possible in cases of a lone perpetrator, who must handle all stress and details himself. On many occasions, through the use of electronic listening and viewing devices, we were able to ascertain that everyone had in fact fallen asleep. Subsequent rescue and capture was then very easy.

Don't Make Suggestions

During the course of your incarceration by a hostage-taker, you may be tempted to make suggestions or give direction to your captor. This is especially true of the perennially "helpful" personality. Try to submerge these impulses. The reason behind this guideline is that if your well-intentioned suggestion should go awry, the captor may think you had tried to trick or deceive him. His reaction may be of a violent nature to "make an example" of you to the other hostages to prevent them from "helping."

Escape? Should You or Shouldn't You

This is a very complex question. Most assuredly, everyone has the right to try for personal survival. Self-preservation is a very powerful and primary drive. In certain instances, where an aircraft remains on the ground, or the hostage incident occurs in a building, people have successfully escaped their captors. In a bank incident in Queens, N.Y., where police had infiltrated the basement, every time a hostage was permitted to visit the toilet they were spirited out of the building to freedom. This was accomplished without the perpetrators' awareness. During a hijacking in the Middle East, a few hostages were able to escape by the tail cone door and flee into the darkness and safety. And on a hijacked airplane in the U.S. while one hijacker was on the flight deck, his female cohort fell asleep and the flight attendants used an elevator to evacuate all the passengers.

It is, of course, a very subjective topic and one that requires careful consideration. In other instances, escapees were caught by the hostage-takers and severely beaten. In the hijacking of a Lufthansa aircraft that ended in Mogadishu, the perpetrators thought that the captain had tried to escape. This was not true, but nonetheless when he returned to the aircraft the hijackers shot and killed him. If the escape attempt is done with great bravado, the hostage-takers may feel that they must demonstrate even greater control over their remaining victims. They may harm or kill them to make public their seriousness to retain control. Though some of these people may be strangers to you, on the other hand you may have friends or family left behind in captivity. While there are still hostages, play it low key and keep any plans for escape quiet. And if you are successful, don't brag about your accomplishment until the incident is over for the remaining hostages.

Attempting an escape is like attempting to broadjump a chasm. If you can jump 8 feet but the distance is 8 feet and 6 inches, you come close but you don't make it. Think about your opportunities and then rethink them again.

Advise on and Request Special Medication or Aid If Needed

If you or one of the other hostages has a medical problem, one which may require medication or special attention, bring it to the attention of the hostage-taker. Wait until the panic has subsided and quietly but directly tell him of these needs. You should tell him once and then not dwell on it or become repetitious. If you become an annoyance or "stand out," it may cause harm to you. They may attempt to capitalize on the special request in their negotiations with authorities. Don't let that worry you, once it is on the "table," they may resolve it in your favor.

Be Observant

Mentally take note of everything you see and hear. After the initial panic subsides, this mental exercise will assist you to cope. Try to memorize things such as: 1) The number of perpetrators, their appearance and conversations. 2) The kinds and numbers of weapons carried. 3) The number of hostages and their identities or descriptions. 4) Where you are being held, and if any routine has settled in. 5) The chain of command, and who is in charge.

On a train hijacking in Bellen, Holland, by South Moluccan terrorists, a hostage, who was a journalist, successfully kept a written journal. This is not a suggested procedure, though, since it may make you "stand out." In a more recent hijacking, one of the victims had a hidden camera and took photographs. Great care and thought should go into this kind of action. If you are released before the other hostages, your information will be invaluable to the authorities in their tactical planning should a later rescue be necessary.

Be Prepared to Speak to the Police on the Telephone

If permitted to speak on the telephone, be prepared to answer questions from the police with a "yes" or "no." If the perpetrators are listening in on the conversation, try to indicate that with a statement such as "Don't lie to us," or "these people can hear what you are saying." If you are forced or required to tell the authorities something you know is a lie or falsehood, you might indicate this by encrypting a statement such as "Have my brother Bob pay my mortgage." The fact that you don't have a brother named Bob will become apparent to the authorities who will be doing a profile on the group of hostages. Also as a matter of policy, all intelligence supplied by any of the hostages must always be verified by the authorities.

Don't Be Argumentative

This pertains to your actions toward the captors, and even to other hostages. Our studies have shown that those individuals who "stand out" or are perceived as a threat, are often singled out by the captors. They may be treated violently, or even killed. Cooperate with your captors—do everything that you are directed to do, short of harming another person, without an argument.

Treat the Captors Like Royalty

This statement means never to turn your back to them,

unless you are directed to do so. Maintain eye contact, but don't stare. This eye contact may facilitate a more rapid development of transference, or the "Stockholm syndrome," which will be detailed later. This can help victim survival, since people are less likely to harm someone they are looking at face-to-face.

It is important to note that this section does not apply to individual kidnappings, the surreptitious holding of a victim. In this case it is best to NEVER LOOK AT THE KIDNAPPER. In a hostage confrontation any number of people involved could identify the perpetrators because of the public nature of the incident. In a kidnapping, however, the victim is the only "eyewitness" and the only person who could link the offender to the crime. If the victim were eliminated, then the suspect would again have anonymity and mobility. After a long period of time, however, even a kidnapper may develop a rapport with his victim.

Be Patient

Be patient even though it may seem that the authorities are doing nothing on your behalf. Most departments will be engaged in a complete program designed to bring you out of this crisis as safely and as quickly as possible. Remember that *time is on your side.* Everyone will get hungry and tired, and the hostage-takers' resolve to continue will diminish. The biological functions of all concerned will work in your favor. In many instances, hostages have been traded for food, drink and/or toilet facilities. There have been some cases in which the captors have surrendered rather than face the indignity of going to the toilet in the presence of others. This would be less likely to happen in a prison environment, where there is generally less privacy, and the perpetrators would be accustomed to these conditions.

Sleep has brought many hostage incidents to a safe conclusion. Physiologically, the stress and anxiety of the situation bears heavily on captors and victims alike. It has not been uncommon for authorities to have to wake everyone up after gaining control of the situation. Some perpetrators have been quite surprised to be awakened, be placed in handcuffs, and several victims have been awakened to the news that "It's OK, it's all over." Sleep, from a psychological standpoint, is an acceptable way for the perpetrator to "surrender" without "losing face." Everyone can identify with being unable to stay awake, and the perpetrator's excuse goes like this: "After all, if I only could have stayed awake, they never would have captured me. I never surrendered."

A Black or Red Passport (Diplomatic And Official, Respectively) Might Not Bring You the Best of Privileges

The exclusivity of walking through immigration or customs, may be far outweighed by the risks should a hostage incident take place. Many ranking officials now carry a blue, tourist passport on their person and leave their official papers in their checked on luggage.

Get Rid of Items That Could Single You Out as a Person Your Captors Might Be Fearful of (police, military, religious or political groups)

Police officers both active and retired should quickly get rid of their badges and credentials as surreptitiously as possible, even between the seats or in some other location. Many federal agents and police now place their credentials in their checked luggage. The carrying of other emblems, both military and religious, can also create problems.

In the Middle East, the Marine Corps' eagle, globe and anchor is considered by many Palestinians as a symbol of U.S. "aggression" against them, and those carrying that emblem or anything like it may be treated with greater harshness. Again in the Middle East, the wearing of a Star of David might also single the person out for specific treatment by certain terrorist organizations. In a free and open society these privileges are taken for granted, but for safety's sake, discretion may be the better part of valor.

If Rescue Comes, Be Prepared to *Hit the Deck!*

A rescue attempt might be indicated by yelling, loud noises such as made by flash grenades, and bright lights. *Get down and stay down.* Cover your head with your hands. Follow the orders of the rescuers without hesitation. Keep your hands in view at all times. Remember, the rescuers may not know who the hostages or the captors are until after they have complete control of the situation. They will treat everyone alike until they can definitely identify the victims. This is especially true in situations where there are large numbers of hostages and perpetrators. The fear is that a captor can escape in the guise of a hostage.

On May 5, 1980, at the rescue of the Iranian Mission in London by the British SAS (Special Air Services), everyone in the mission was handled very roughly. Some persons were even handcuffed. All people removed from the Mission were thrust from trooper to trooper, to the rear yard of the mission where they were forced to lie face down on the grass. This was done quite unceremoniously, but the reasoning was sound. The rescuers knew there had been at least six perpetrators. Five had been identified and shot during the assault. The sixth, and possibly others, was still unidentified. Procedure requires that the assault force maintain "total control." This minimizes the danger of an unexpected gunfight where not only the rescuers but also the hostages could be injured. This will be expanded upon later.

Who Could Become a Hostage?

Who could become victim of a hostage taking? The answer is almost anyone, but some jobs and types of employment have a greater probability. Highest on the list of victims of the "professional criminal" (types of hostage-takers will be discussed in a later chapter) are bank employees and retail sales persons. Willie Sutton, a notorious bank robber in New York during the 1940's and 1950's, when asked why he robbed banks, replied, "Because that's where the money is." We are living at a

time when domestic terrorist groups and other extremists have targeted banks and armored cars to assist in the
funding of their causes. They, too, are going "where the
money is."

"Frequent fliers," are offered a great many induce-
ments, benefits and prizes to fly often on certain
airlines—everything from upgrading of tickets to free
flights around the world. But there is another less desirable award—the greater statistical possibility of being on
board a plane that is hijacked. (This does not mean you
should stop flying. After all, many more people are killed
or injured on a holiday weekend on our nation's high-
ways than have been killed or injured during all of the
contemporary acts of terrorism in the past two decades.)
Should it happen to you, our easily remembered 15
points may help you to cope with and exit the ordeal
without injury or permanent psychological trauma.

Those in management of businesses or enterprises are
often the targets of acts of terrorism. A disgruntled employee, a former employee, a stockholder or any group
with a real or imagined grievance could single out your
company for punishment. Even as a co-worker you could
be caught up in the action. Corporate executives and expatriate employees in politically unstable areas of the
world face a greater risk of being kidnapped or taken
hostage. Awareness, training and the taking of some basic precautions can reduce this risk tremendously.

If you are a "non-corporate" reader, don't let yourself
be lulled into a sense of false security, for hostage inci-

dents can and have occurred to the shopping housewife, the office worker, the student and the vacationer.

Even travelers who are on vacation or sabbatical may be at risk. It could happen on an aircraft, a motorbus or a cruise ship, as the incident involving the ship the *Achille Lauro* most recently demonstrated. Tourists all over the globe seem to be very vulnerable, especially if they travel to certain countries or areas where turmoil exists. But even in these areas, statistically your chances of being taken are slight, and you can minimize them further. Check out the area you intend to travel to. This information is available from the State Department's Travelers Hotline at (202) 647-5225. If your plans to visit an area correspond to a "significant date" (i.e., revolutionary anniversary, massacre, etc.), a time when violent actions may be taken to call attention to that date, then you might consider avoiding that area at that time.

Who might be singled out? Among a group of passengers, it might well be the Americans or our Western Allies. In these times of surrogate warfare, Americans particularly have become pawns in what Brian Jenkins of the Rand Corporation has termed "The Theater of Terror." The terrorists are the stars, the hostages are the supporting cast, and the entire world the audience.

The actions and ideologies of terrorists are reported, analyzed, magnified and at times almost glorified by the media. Any one of us could find himself in the midst of this "media event." Anyone can wander into a robbery in progress, a family or domestic dispute, or a lovers' triangle. Anyone can be in the "wrong place at the wrong time." The possibilities are endless.

The Hostage-Taker's Family

In addition to "who" could be taken, let's examine the role or dilemma of the family and loved ones of the hostage-taker. The notification will often take the form of police officers looking for information about the offender. They will attempt to learn of his background, motivations or peculiarities. Another mode of notification may come from seeing the incident on TV, or receiving a call from friend or neighbor after they hear of it. One of the first feelings will be one of shock, and this then many times turns to feelings of anger and embarrassment.

Usually the first action of the family will be to try and get to the scene as quickly as possible, with the thought that they can "talk some sense" into the perpetrator before things get worse. We have found that on many occasions it is the relationship with the family or loved one that has contributed to the situation in the first place. The introduction of the wife or mother may further excite or inflame the perpetrator into actions. He may try to impress them that "they made me do this" or "they pushed me too far." This is the audience he is playing to, and when they show up at the scene, "the show must go on." As in many suicide attempts, the purpose is to put guilt on the loved one. The remorse for this "trouble I put you through," and the thought that "you'll be better off after I'm gone" may prompt some individuals to prove their intentions.

There are some agencies and departments that feel they shouldn't obstruct the family from speaking to the hostage-taker. Some feel that if it worked in a James Cagney movie, it is worth a try. Also, if something does go wrong, they can wash their hands if "even his mother and a priest couldn't handle him." The responsibility to negotiate and to "bring them back alive" is that of law enforcement, and cannot be delegated.

In New York City it was our decision not to use the wife, family, clergy or media to negotiate. We felt strongly in the law enforcement's responsibility to bring a safe conclusion to these incidents, and do not believe in delegating this responsibility. We do, however, value any information and intelligence gained from speaking to these individuals about the perpetrator.

Many times the media will be utilized by law enforcement agencies, but they should not be involved in negotiations. In their capacity as neutral "watchdog," they can assure no undue harm will come to the perpetrator. In many interviews with former hostage-takers, it was found that they sincerely believed the police would shoot them as they surrendered. By pointing to the media presence, we were able to convince offenders that they would not be beaten or shot, and that they could also make their statements to the ever present TV cameras.

What Situations Can Create a Hostage Incident?

The circumstances can range from making a deposit in a bank, shopping, flying on a business or vacation trip, or merely being at work when a former employee comes in with a grievance. There is little preventative action that you as an individual can take to affect most of these circumstances. Your own conduct will often affect only yourself and your immediate family.

We have seen incidents develop such as the rash of hijackings to Cuba in the early 1980's. Many of those who came to the United States on the boat-lift became disenchanted. Without sufficient funds, and without the desire to repeat that manner of passage, many took the easy route "home." Gasoline, bombs or bogus weapons usually accomplished this, and the hijackings usually proceeded quickly and without violence. In most cases it was merely a slight inconvenience. Your passive conduct will usually be the best response to these situations.

On the other hand, there are certain areas in the world where political unrest creates an extremely high vulnerability for airline passengers. Care must be taken to avoid these areas by careful planning of travel itineraries. This is especially true of pleasure trips and vacations. It may be best to let the unrestful situation "cool down" before venturing into the thick of things. For the business traveler there are various security newsletters which give information on problems and extenuating circumstances in the various areas of the world. These include Ackerman and Palumbo, and the Terrorism Intelligence Report. They have been prepared to assist the international business traveler to stay clear of trouble spots. Awareness, coupled with a little caution, can be a worthwhile preventative measure.

The holiday traveler can find out about problem areas from the State Department, the International Air Transportation Association (IATA) or from a reputable travel agent. Remember that the Chamber of Commerce of the area you are inquiring about is not likely to tell you about the crime at the hotels or recreation spots of that area, since it might very well discourage tourism to their cities or countries if it were known.

The presence of an angry employee or former employee is often noted in the workplace, but few people would think of calling security or management. The fear of embarrassment many times prevents these steps, but it becomes a mistake that can and has proven fatal. In one instance several employees observed a suspended employee park his car and then remove several rifles and handguns from his trunk. They were so fascinated by this sight that none thought of calling the police until he had fired a few shots. At the end of this incident, four persons were dead and another three were seriously wounded. Often it takes time for our minds to analyze what our eyes have seen, and then to bring about the proper response. Prompt action could make the difference in this kind of situation.

A robbery in a bank or retail establishment, and the unexpectedly rapid response of the police, can create an unexpected confrontation between the perpetrator and the authorities. The criminal panics and goes through a "fight or flight" reaction. With his escape now blocked, he takes innocent bystanders to use as a "ticket to freedom." That expression was so often used in incidents we handled, we thought that perhaps the criminals were attending seminars to learn the right things to say.

Remember that during the panic of the first few minutes of an incident you are in grave danger. Follow the subject's instructions very quickly. The slightest hesitation may be interpreted as resistance or a threat, and he may then harm you.

When and Where Do Hostage Situations Take Place?

These situations may occur at any time, depending on what precipitates the incident. At the business establishment robbery, if it is a real "criminal incident," the situation may arise when the culprit's escape is blocked by the arrival of Law Enforcement personnel. If it is an individual with an inadequate self-image, his entire plan and program may be to take a "high visibility" person to draw attention to himself or his cause. For this person, stamping his feet or banging his head against a wall has not gotten him the exposure he desires. He feels the grandstand gesture of a hostage taking will "prove" his seriousness.

Another person may take hostage a family member or someone to influence his spouse or lover, and thereby prove his devotion. Still another and more frequent family crisis centers around the custody of a child. The situation may reach crisis proportions when custody is granted to the other parent, or revoked by the courts. Daily, in newspapers, on television and on milk cartons, we see photos of children who are "missing." Many of these children were "successfully" abducted by an estranged parent, without the intervention of the authorities. Many of these were potential hostage situations, and may still develop as such if the other parent locates them. We have spent many hours on rooftops with distraught fathers dangling their child or themselves over the edge of a roof.

Aircraft hijackings usually occur just after take-off, if the plane is not headed where the perpetrator desires to go, or just prior to landing. This latter is often done so the plane can be diverted before the formalities of landing take place.

Bank robberies used to take place just prior to the bank's opening for business. Entry was gained by following or forcing an employee into the bank as he reported for work. Nowadays, there is no "scheduling," so any time you are in a bank, you could be vulnerable. The less time you need to spend in the bank, the less the possibility of becoming involved in an incident. One way to cut down on your time in the bank would be to do your paperwork beforehand. Make out deposit or withdrawal slips at home or in the office before entering the bank. A simple but obvious way of avoiding trouble would be to glance through the doors or windows before entering the bank. If you notice everyone laying on the floor while gunmen are emptying the drawers, then obviously you should avoid joining the situation.

In the workplace, a poor corporate public image can often affect vulnerability. This is not limited to expatriate corporations in foreign countries. Corporations in the U.S. engaged in business with countries that are "unpopular," such as South Africa, Iran or Libya, could prove to be targets. Utilities, especially nuclear power plants, have found themselves adversaries to individuals or organizations who are or purport to be environmentally motivated. An individual who was an animal lover took hostages in an animal rescue center in New York State to call attention to the animals who might have to be destroyed.

You owe it to yourself, your colleagues and your employer to maintain awareness of persons, things or incidents which are unusual and possibly hazardous.

Abortion clinics and planned parenthood centers have proven to be targets of "well-intentioned bombers." These locations could very well be the sites of future hostage incidents to call attention to the ongoing dispute of "pro-life" and "pro-choice."

In this democratic society many foreign nationals and those emigrating here have brought with them their long-standing animosities and hatreds. They have used these shores and this country as their battleground. This has been evidenced by such terrorist acts on behalf of the Croatians vs. the Yugoslavs, the Armenians vs. the Turks, the Anti-Castro Cubans vs. the Pro-Castro Cubans, and the Pakistani-backed Sikhs vs. Indian moslems. Some of these terrorist acts have erupted at airports, travel agencies, office buildings, diplomatic legations, shopping malls and even fast-food restaurants.

Even being a passenger on a bus can prove hazardous. In Jasper, Arkansas, two religious fanatics held 15 people hostage for hours before committing suicide. On an interstate bus that eventually ended up at Kennedy Airport in New York, a paranoid sailor shot and killed two people, and then wounded two others before contact was made, and some nine hours later he was negotiated to surrender without any additional casualties.

It was reported that in the incident in 1985 involving the cruise ship *Achille Lauro*, the hijacking took place when the terrorists were discovered by some of the crew. They were allegedly using the ship as a means of transportation to conduct terrorist acts on Israeli shores. Once discovered, the terrorists *prematurely* sprang into action *at an inopportune time.* Although the ship had not been the original target, with the media attention accorded it, you can be sure that a ship like it will be tried again in the future.

And now, some special circumstances involving aircraft. Generally speaking, in the event of an aircraft emergency, aisle seats offer better opportunity for escape. They also offer more convenience to use facilities, and usually a bit more elbow room under normal flight conditions albeit without the panoramic views of window seats. The seats at the emergency window exits (on those craft containing them) usually offer several inches of additional space and legroom. This can add to comfort as well as facilitating an easier exit, should that be required. Most airlines, by law or practice, will not assign window exit seats to children. In the event of an emergency they might not be capable of opening the window hatch.

In one of his publications, the consumer advocate Ralph Nader advised selecting the escape window row. If that were not available, he advised to count the backs of seats from your seat to the closest emergency door or window. In the event of an emergency with darkness or smoke, you could "feel" your way to the emergency exit by counting seat backs. In the recent rescue attempt by Egyptian commandos in Malta, most of the hostages died of smoke inhalation in the ensuing fire, possibly because they were unable to exit the aircraft.

However, in the event of a hijacking, the aisle seat might create more of a problem than a convenience. This seat offers greater contact with the hijacker, and chance for more interaction. This accessibility can put you in more jeopardy in that you might be selected as an "example," or you might be perceived as a threat. Should a hijacking take place, try to blend in with your surroundings as much as possible. If you are defiant or threatening, they may try to neutralize your threat by harming or killing you. If you are overly submissive, they may select you as an "easy mark" and likewise feel safe making an example of you to guarantee compliance by the other hostages. On most flights the window seat will insulate you both physically and psychologically from the perpetrators.

On overseas flights it is suggested that the following points should be considered: a) Fly an American carrier on a direct route to your destination, even if this means altering your time schedule. (I always fly on a U.S. carrier, because in an emergency I want to hear the announcement in a language I understand. I don't want to have to wait for the translation.) If you must travel in Europe or the Middle East, then the more secure airlines of El Al, SAS or Swissair are suggested because of their safety records. b) When checking in at the airport, arrive early and check in at the secure area right away. This is usually beyond the x-ray and metal detector areas, and will lessen your time of vulnerability. Even in these secure spaces it is wise to avoid the areas where storage lockers are located, and locations with large glass windows.

In most bombings more people were injured or killed by the secondary shrapnel (flying glass and metal from lockers) than the primary blast from the bomb. The incident at LaGuardia Airport, where 11 people died on December 17, 1975, when a bomb exploded, would be a prime example, as would the ones at DaVinci Airport in

Rome and the Vienna Airport. Though there were many casualties from the direct blasts, many more people were seriously injured from secondary shrapnel.

The statement "Hurt one, scare 1,000; kill one, scare 10,000," is very true. It would be tragic if you were that one individual.

Hijackings and Trickery

The question of using trickery against hijackers comes up often. This action will most often depend on the individual. As a general rule I do not recommend it. If the ruse is discovered, the captors may respond with a great deal of violence.

In the hijacking of TWA flight 847, one passenger said that he feigned blindness by having his wife lead him up and down the aisle between his seat and the lavatory. Whether this worked in his favor or not is an assumption based on his safe release. Reactions of captors can be unpredictable. Just recently in the hijacking of the ship

Achille Lauro, the captors executed an elderly wheelchair-bound man. He may have been selected by them because of his physical condition, but who can say with any certainty.

I recall the old story of an American flyer who was shot down behind enemy lines in France during World War II. He was picked up by the French underground who successfully hid him for three years. He lived openly in public, working in a butcher shop, but since he spoke no French he acted the part of a deaf mute.

Think very seriously before you decide on this type of action. The outcome will depend on your ability to act convincingly during a stressful situation, and even the best actor would have difficulty with the uncertain nature of the players.

How Hostage Situations Happen

If in the process of a robbery the police respond before the perpetrator has made an escape, he will many times take a hostage in an effort to bargain for escape and freedom. He wants out. Some persons have blamed police agencies for too rapid a response as being the causal factor. They feel that if the response did not come as quickly, then the criminals would escape without there being a hostage incident.

Law Enforcement spends large amounts of time and money, exploring ways to be more efficient in communications and response to crime. For Law Enforcement to respond slowly to a robbery would be ludicrous. The author has experienced that proper training to insure quick response with good observation and tactical technique can prevent Law Enforcement from creating hostage incidents, and still effectively arrest the offenders.

In other incidents perpetrators may "stage" a criminal event and await the arrival of the police to commence the action. In some cases the media is the true hostage in what Brian Jenkins of the Rand Corporation termed the "Theater of Terror." The perpetrator is the star, the hostage the supporting cast, and the public and police are the audience.

Many incidents have occurred at court houses when the defendant is returned for sentencing. Cohorts or family members have sneaked weapons or explosives into the courtroom in an attempt to "break-out" their colleague or loved one. One recent example occurred in France in early January of 1986, another case at the Hall of Justice in Bogotá, Columbia, in late 1985. These were extreme cases. The former case was resolved without loss of life, the latter unfortunately was not.

Many times during the legal processes of divorce and child custody hearings, the unsatisfied spouse or guardian may forcibly take the child right there and then, creating a confrontation. They may feel that this hostage incident will demonstrate their love for the child, or their frustration with the workings of the legal system. What really can happen, can be very dangerous to all persons involved. Sometimes the untimely or injudicious response of police officers to a simple family dispute can explode into a hostage drama, with anyone nearby caught up in the tide of events.

Types of Hostage-Takers

In order for you to have a better understanding of the types of persons who would take hostages, in perhaps an oversimplification we have grouped them into three very broad categories.

The first is the *professional criminal*. This refers not to the classic jewel thief on the Riviera in tuxedo and white gloves, but to the individual who sustains himself through repeated thievery and a life of crime. Through chance encounter, or unexpected confrontation with Law Enforcement officials, he becomes a hostage-taker as he looks for a means of escape. He might reach out to anyone around him for use as a shield, to save himself from police action. Once again, the first few minutes of this confrontation put you in extremely grave danger. The perpetrator may panic as he finds himself weighing a chance to flee, or stay and fight off the police. During this time, more police officers are killed than at any other time in a confrontation. And you are now in the middle. Follow orders. Do not resist unless you are absolutely certain you can succeed.

After the initial panic subsides, the professional criminal becomes the easiest perpetrator for the police to deal with. He will recognize his dilemma and will usually be rational, opting for whatever deal he can strike. When this happens, he will usually look to the hostages for a way out. He may seek support and advice on how to safely conclude the situation. He will try to work out the best deal he can, but he is usually aware of the fact that he won't escape completely. Often the most he will hope for is his own bodily safety.

As more time passes, the likelihood that the perpetrator will harm you decreases. The bond that will form between both of you will be almost imperceptible at first. Cooperation with the captor is usually not a conscious decision. As the ordeal lengthens, it will appear that it is you and he against the world outside. This phenomenon is known as transference. It is a very strong identification between individuals who are sharing a crisis, and like it or not, you as the victim are in fact sharing in the goals of the hostage-taker. Wisely, the authorities do not discourage its development. It may seem to you, however, that they are ignoring you—the victim—and are only concerned with the criminal. Remember that if they solve his problem, they solve yours. This is discussed in greater detail later.

One of the dangers with this type of captor is that he may believe that as he exits he will be shot or that when apprehended receive an even worse punishment. The bravado from old prison movies, "They'll never take me alive," may cause him to opt for suicide instead of incarceration. If he lacks the conviction to kill himself, he may act in such a way as to draw fire from the authorities, hurting the hostages or going out in a blaze of gunfire. This would make the police instruments in his own suicide, and possibly would endanger you. You may encourage him to opt for surrender since the hostage-negotiating teams are trained not to shoot unless absolutely necessary.

The second type of hostage-taker is the *emotionally disturbed person*. He may be psychotic or have an *unstable personality*. He may be an individual who cannot cope with family or work problems, or a psychopath who is completely out of touch with reality. By and large, the greatest number of hostage situations involve these individuals. Domestic squabbles, custody cases, disgruntled employees or a grievance with some authority can push them over the edge. These situations are extremely difficult for the negotiator as well as for the hostage. The anxiety level and many times the rationality of the subject may ride up and down like a rollercoaster. He will be prone to explosive outbursts and irrational behavior that will raise the levels of fear and anxiety in yourself and possibly the law enforcement negotiator. The techniques used by negotiators are anxiety-reduction procedures, and are applied under the basic principle that "The life of the hostage is the most important goal."

The last category of hostage-taker is the *politically motivated terrorist.* While the emotionally disturbed captor may account for more frequent seizures, it is this class of captor that gets the most exposure. That, in fact, is often the hidden agenda for the captors, to publish their list of grievances, or to force some government or authority group into fulfilling their goals. One need look only to the newspapers or the evening news to see where some group in Central America or the Middle East have captured a group of innocents to give the terrorist the upper hand in some ideological battle. Closer to home, "underground" groups, prisoners who "have nothing to lose" or religious fanatics may not take your life that seriously, since they will gladly give up theirs for the "cause," and yours as well.

Islamic and religious fundamentalists consider Israel their enemy and the United States an instrument of the Zionist cause. These groups offer the greatest immediate concern to government and law enforcement agencies, both at home and abroad. The Ayatollah Khomeini and Colonel Muammar Qaddafi have both targeted westerners, especially Americans, for the brunt of their nationalistic propaganda and action. Their quarrels may be with the policies of the government, but they will hold citizens hostage in this surrogate warfare.

Mohammed, the prophet who established Islam and brought the word of Allah through the Koran, was extremely tolerant of other religions. He called Jews and the Christians "people of the book" (the Bible) and identified Moses and Jesus as prophets. Contrary to his teachings, many of today's leaders are not as tolerant of other Judeo-Christian people or governments.

For those who are motivated by religious fervor, there can be no rationalization by argument. They cannot bargain away their beliefs and therefore are the most difficult group to negotiate with. However, in many instances, the containment of these people and the application of time may tend to reduce the psychological reinforcement that some individuals require. The resolve to "die for the cause" looks less and less appealing, and the desire to "live and fight another day" becomes more acceptable and honorable. Instead of being carried out in a box as a martyr, they can be carried on their colleagues' shoulders as heroes.

Coping with Long-Term Incarceration

Ambassador Bruce Langdon, one of the Americans held for 444 days in the U.S. Mission in Iran, sums it up with, "Humans are like teabags, you don't know how strong they are until they get into hot water."

If you are in an occupation or profession where because of vocation or location you may be vulnerable to kidnapping, some personal "pre-incident planning" is crucial. Knowing that your affairs are in order, that your family and loved ones will be safe and provided for, will permit you to cope with your immediate problems.

For our example of dealing with long-term incarceration, we can give credit to Sir Geoffrey Jackson. As British Ambassador in Montevideo, Uruguay, he was kidnapped on January 8, 1971, by the Tupamaros, a local terrorist group. He was one of the first individuals to successfully survive a nine-month captivity in a "people's prison." To get through the ordeal, he coped both physically and psychologically. He utilized the then-popular Canadian Airforce Exercise Program daily to maintain physical strength and cardiovascular well-being. To overcome the mental anguish of his long captivity, he maintained a dignified and conscious identity as the British Ambassador. He kept a rough calendar to stay oriented. Even marks on a wall can help you keep track of the days. At one point, to reinforce his identity, he wrote out on a large piece of paper a chart or "Magna Carta" with the following points:

1) This is *not* a "people's prison."
2) To the contrary, this is the British Embassy so long as I remain in it.
3) I am *not* the people's prisoner.
4) To the contrary, I am unjustly held captive, being guilty of no offense against any man.
5) I represent in this place a great and honorable nation, which is a force wholly for good in the world.

Another very important part of his facility for coping was that he did not have to worry about his family. When he became aware of a possible, pending kidnapping, Sir Geoffrey made an agreement with his wife, Lady

Jackson. In essence the pact was that if he were taken, she was to pack two bags, one for him and one for herself. She was to leave Sir Geoffrey's bag at the embassy, and she was to proceed to England to their summer cottage and supervise its painting. Sir Geoffrey, being fully aware that Lady Jackson would comply with the agreement, knew that he need only worry about himself during the incarceration.

Similar arrangements between members of other families who might be vulnerable, would definitely make the trauma of captivity more bearable, should it occur.

Diego Ascendio, our ambassador to Colombia, disagrees somewhat in being a passive hostage. On February 27, 1980, he was taken hostage at a diplomatc function at the embassy of the Dominican Republic in Bogota, Columbia. Ascendio found himself held hostage with about 14 other ambassadors among a group of more than 50 captives. These ambassadors, whose function it was to negotiate for their governments, almost without thought assumed that role in this situation. Their captors, though educated revolutionaries, were not schooled in the principles of negotiation. When they were going to send out their list of demands, Ambassador Ascendio and others persuaded their captors to let them edit and modify the demands in the hopes they would not receive a flat refusal. In one sense this is beneficial in that it precluded the captors from total frustration which might have led to aggression against the hostages. On the other hand, the government negotiators were now dealing with terrorists who had some of the best tutorial assistance available in the world. This included almost all of the nearly 15 ambassadors. Only the Israeli ambassador chose not to get directly involved.

These actions kept Ascendio and the others busy and gave them something to occupy their time. Things became so cordial inside the embassy that some countries sent in special food and champagne. Note that the champagne almost caused a rift among the non-diplomatic hostages who thought the ambassadors were not going to share the festive bubbly. Eventually on April 27, 1980, after some concessions, the hostages were released.

The psychological commitment to survival is absolutely imperative. This can be accomplished in many ways:

Remain flexible.

Control your fears and anxiety levels. You are worth more alive than dead.

Have patience and courage, even during the times when your captors may be trying to demoralize you.

Maintain your self-respect, even as difficult as it may seem. With some psychotic kidnappers and terrorists, pleading for mercy will only encourage annoyance or perhaps more sadistic treatment.

The importance of not giving in or giving up cannot be overemphasized. In 1986 in Columbia two men were kidnapped. They were kept isolated except for one hour each day when they were allowed to see and speak to each other. One man was in great despair over their situation, and both prisoners were unaware that the arrangements to pay their ransom had been made. As the mechanics of the payment were being worked out, the disheartened prisoner (almost on the very day the ransom was paid) lay down and died of "natural causes." He had just given up all hope.

It cannot be emphasized too much that pre-incident psychological preparations are imperative for all persons who could become long-term kidnap victims. Remember, the targets are not limited to businessmen and diplomats. As we have seen in Lebanon, the clergy, media and academicians have also become targets.

Moorhead Kennedy, also a hostage held in Iran for 444 days, said, "There are not many atheists among hostages." He also remarked that you needed the following to survive: Humor, Optimism, Patience, Energy, (H.O.P.E.).

Media

Dealing with the media might be the last thing you would think about while preparing to embark on a business trip or vacation, unless you are in public relations. But make no mistake about it, should you or a member of your family be kidnapped or taken hostage, you will find yourself thrust headlong into the media jungle.

If you are taken hostage in a short-term incident, such as a robbery or employee dispute, the local TV, radio and print media will cover the story in great detail. They will want to interview you upon your release, and will ask a great many questions concerning the episode. Some of these questions will be appropriate, some utterly ridiculous and others very insensitive. Media people are just regular people, with the same failings and foibles as the rest of us, so don't expect too much. The difference is that we see and hear a lot more of them than our friends and families, so we often give them a special regard. For the most part they are not trained negotiators, and many of them have never covered the "police beat," so they have little insight into the nuances of hostage negotiating. Despite this there have been some reporters who have felt their "neutrality" has given them a better position and insight into the hostage situation.

Because of this limited understanding, there were many incidents this author negotiated where the media would telephone the hostage site and attempt to interview the participants. This would tie up telephone lines and either prolong or hamper our efforts to resolve the situation. To deal with this dangerous type of interference, often physical action was necessitated, such as chopping the phone line with an ax. Subsequently, cooperation from the telephone company eliminated the need for such extreme measures. We understand that the reporters and assignment editors meant for no harm to come to the captives. They were interested in what they thought would help the situation, while preserving the goal of reporting the news first, fast and if possible with an "exclusive."

But the media does interfere, ranging from a Canadian reporter telling the hostage-taker that if he exchanged all his hostages for narcotics he'd have nothing left to bargain with to a Washington, D.C., talkshow host asking if the perpetrator thought he could trust the police, and the seeds of doubt sown can jeopardize the lives of all involved. In one of the latest situations, at Van Cleef and Arpels in Beverly Hills, a representative from UPI and Mutual Broadcast News spoke with the hostage-taker and hostage while the incident was going on. When an incident is concluded and everyone is released unharmed, many times the media will believe that they have contributed to the outcome in spite of what the police authorities may say. But in the Beverly Hills incident, three people died, two after the media communicated inside with the principals. What effect they had in this case may be decided in a Civil Court.

In a kidnap incident in New York City in 1979, Metromedia Broadcasting was sued in a similar situation. In essence, the complaint stated that a News Team followed and filmed the banker-husband of a hostage making a ransom drop, and placed the victim in greater danger had they been observed by the kidnappers. Though the ransom was paid and the victim was recovered physically unharmed, it is reported that an out-of-court settlement was agreed upon.

Whether or not you should give an interview to the media is entirely up to you. Most mental health professionals who deal with the field of victimology agree that an interview can be part of the ventilation process. This is an important catharsis to relieve the anxiety and emotion after such a trying experience. Likewise, some of the former hostages I have spoken with indicated that they felt better after they sat down and wrote out what had happened to them. The ventilating has apparently helped more than one former hostage get their lives "back on track."

If your capture or imprisonment involves an international or unusual national situation, the major networks may vie for your presence and interviews. After the recent hijacking of TWA flight 847, with its Mediterranean odyssey back and forth to Beirut, the American hostages became household names and media regulars on "Good Morning America," "Nightline" and all of the other networks as well.

The electronic media has been accused of "television diplomacy," even to the extent that they brought about the "snap election" in the Philippines that eventually brought about the fall of President Marcos.

While this assumption may embellish its role, it cannot be denied that the media has an especially sensitive role in kidnappings and terrorist actions.

In a long-term incarceration or kidnapping, the families of victims may be skyrocketed into national media prominence, especially if they have good "stage presence" and interview well. They may find themselves on the circuit, from early morning to late-night talk shows, in all manner of electronic and print media. It has been learned that in politically motivated kidnappings, research into the potential victims' families was done to ascertain whether or not they would be effective in putting pressure on the company or government to comply with the demands of the captors.

Many of the families of the American hostages held for 444 days in Iran became well versed in the operations of the media. It has been speculated that the attention accorded the families, and the hostage incident itself, contributed to the downfall of the Carter Administration.

It is true that when our own families or loved ones are involved, we may willingly violate every principle of negotiation or national diplomatic policy. We must be aware, however, that many times the families are being manipulated by the captors. Any of their violations of these policies will not necessarily bring about the safe or expedient release of their loved ones. This is especially true if the captors see that they can divide public opinion on their behalf. They are in no rush, as time is on their side and their casts are kept to a minimum with the volunteer help of people dedicated to "the cause." And often, as we have seen, the families and media become secondary hostages, delivering the messages of the captors.

The Do's and Don'ts

During the course of your captivity, whether it be long (weeks or months) or comparatively short (hours or days), there are certain types of conduct that would not be appropriate or safe.

In many incidents, during the confusion of the initial takeover, many people have simply walked away from their would-be captors. The avenue of escape presented itself, and they took advantage of it. It is difficult to predict when such an opportunity might arise, or in what manner it might present itself. Often as not, it is a matter of chance. But it is the situation when that conduit is

closed that we will concern ourselves with here. After
the initial panic has subsided, you and your fellow captives (if you have been taken with others) will have to
think of how to conclude this nightmare.

The Right of Everyone for Personal Survival Is Paramount

If you are tempted to escape, some consideration should
be given as to how it will be accomplished. Try to take
into account your chances of success. (The analogy of
broad-jumping 8 feet across an 8½ foot chasm holds
true—close but no cigar. You didn't make it.) Another
thing to consider is the likelihood of punishment for an
unsuccessful escape attempt. This was touched upon in
an earlier chapter.

Resorting to Trickery

In a recent hijacking, a passenger resorted to trickery in
that he feigned blindness. He and his wife were permitted to leave the aircraft safely. Apparently the terrorists considered them a nuisance. Not everyone is
equipped to successfully carry off such a ruse. You must
consider your capabilities and whether or not you think
your captors would be so amiable to a handicapped hostage. We have seen, unfortunately, harsh treatment
against such "weaker" hostages to set examples of the resolve and ruthlessness of the captors. REMEMBER if
you are successful in this manner of escape, don't boast

of your accomplishment until the rest of the hostages are safe. They could suffer harsh consequences because of your success and their feelings of failure.

Overpowering the Captors

A recently aired television special depicted an aircraft hijacking. At the end of the program, after having suffered many acts of terror and violence, the passengers overpowered and captured the hostage-takers and considered vigilante justice. These actions make great TV and movie fare, but when the show is over everyone can get up and go home. When it comes to drama or realism in Hollywood or on TV, drama always wins out.

Here are some real things to consider: How many perpetrators are there? You might be able to surprise and overcome one, but if there are other captors can you count on the support of the other hostages? Even trained sharpshooters, when faced with the necessity of using deadly force, have experienced a moment of hesitation. Fellow passengers may not be dependable if you need their help in overpowering your captors. Also consider your location in the aircraft. You may not be able to safely communicate your intentions to fellow captives without the repression and counteractions of additional hijackers.

Another consideration is the type of weaponry the hijackers may be equipped with. Handguns and automatic weapons can be devastating enough, but at 35,000 feet in a pressurized cabin they can be exceptional. The explosion and depressurization aboard TWA flight 840 in 1986 saw four persons sucked from the aircraft to their deaths, and that was at only 15,000 feet. Explosives and grenades can cause blast and shrapnel damage, but may also ignite fires in the aircraft. The recent Egyptian Airlines hijacking, in November of 1985, and the subsequent rescue attempt underscored this danger. Of the 60 persons killed during the episode, most died during the rescue attempt when exploding grenades caused fires in the cabin.

Humor

During short-term incarceration it would not be in your best interests to engage in humor. During the initial takeover the captors are trying to instill fear and obtain compliance on the part of the victims. Joking may indicate that you are not taking them seriously, and they may feel compelled to demonstrate their power by hurting you. In addition, remember you don't want to "stand out" by exceptional behavior or the hijackers may single you out as an example. As the ordeal drags on and the "Stockholm syndrome" (transference) takes hold, humor may ease the tension on the part of all involved. Care must be taken on the subject matter of the humor. Ethnic or religious humor which denigrates a group or sect may play into the hands of those trying to test the attitudes of their captives. You would be wise to be careful in your acknowledgment of or participation in this subject matter.

In a long-term incarceration, as in an individual kidnap situation by professional or political kidnappers, there could well be a place for humor. In many incidents the guards of the victim were just about as captive as their charge. They experienced boredom, anxiety and fear of capture. In the interaction and development of the "Stockholm syndrome," as just stated, humor can act as a good catalyst, encouraging the coping mechanisms of all concerned.

Games or Contests

In the course of an extended captivity, often, to pass the time, the captors or guards may suggest games of cards, checkers or chess with their victims. Many times those persons who are employed or utilized to guard you may be of a decidedly lower I.Q. than yourself. With little effort you may be able to "beat the pants off" them. This will only serve to embarrass the guards and may bring about some form of reprisal to show "who is boss." It is suggested that should you engage in this type of activity to pass the time, that you not overwhelm or defeat your opponent. Again, diplomats and those in the foreign service, who are instilled with the need to win for their government, may look at this differently, so you must make this decision. I would be a hardworking but "good loser." Embarrassing my captor would not be in my best interests.

Eye Contact

In a "confrontational" hostage or hijacking situation, we suggest that eye contact would be beneficial in establishing a favorable relationship with your captors. Showing that you are a person and not a mere object would accelerate the facilitation of the transference mentioned before. Remember that hostage and hijacking situations are different from kidnapping situations. In a short-term situation, such as kidnapping of bank managers or criminal abduction, it is suggested that you don't even look at your captors. Measures such as covering your eyes and indicating to them that you don't know who they are or what they look like, so you will not be able to identify them or even describe them to the authorities, may help your survival. Kidnappers are differentiated from the hijacker and hostage-taker in that they have "mobility and anonymity." The only person who might identify them is the victim, and therefore he is in grave danger. In many of the cases researched, the abductors had "dug the hole and bought the quicklime," even before writing the ransom note.

Still you can, as Sir Geoffrey Jackson wrote in a long-term situation, "survive the long night" if you take some of these precautions. Try never to lose your personal dignity. Maintain proper decorum, as difficult as that may sound, especially while experiencing the "panic reaction," the "why me?" and "I don't believe this is really happening" feeling. All are attempts at coping with the enormity and the terror of the situation.

In many political kidnapping situations, especially with terrorist groups who are trying to quickly demoralize their captives, the perpetrators may resort to dynamic actions such as stripping the hostages totally naked, reducing them to an infantile state. They may even require female hostages to strip themselves, to further gain a psychological advantage over their victims. Hostages may then be cast into a dank, bleak cell, illuminated more often than not with a single bare bulb hanging from the ceiling. Perhaps it will even be totally dark, to further demoralize the victim. After all, who knows what horrors can exist in the dark? If cast into a "people's prison," which may be nothing more than a root cellar in a "safe house," terrible horrors can be conjured up in one's own mind. Many times the only provision for hygiene is a hole in the floor, or a rusty pail. These are the psychological ploys used to break the spirit, and make the job of the captor and jailer easier. Often they will try to use you or your statements made under such duress for political purposes. Don't concern yourself with these problems, just be concerned with getting out alive. The world accepts statements made under duress as just that.

Both Sir Geoffrey Jackson and Moorhead Kennedy (the U.S. Diplomat held 444 days in Tehran) were able to maintain dignified and self-assured demeanors. They eventually wore down their captors, and both were able to survive and make their time of incarceration a little more bearable. This may be a trait of those in the diplomatic service, but their experience may be useful to non-diplomatic hostages as well.

The Stockholm Syndrome

This term has been used and abused, understood as well as misunderstood, and has taken on many different definitions. The syndrome itself is nothing more than a coping mechanism which is as involuntary as breathing. It never has, nor should it ever have, any negative connotations. The phenomena is parallel to the psychological term "transference." Transference refers to the relationship that forms between patient and doctor, which permits the therapy to be successful. The patient must believe that the therapist can help him in order for the treatment to meet with success. The patient usually becomes an evangelist for the therapist, telling anyone who will listen what a great doctor he is and how he can help them with their problems. Mental health professionals have labelled this as the "therapeutic honeymoon," where the therapist can do no wrong. However, this period lasts only about six months, and then what was positive becomes negative as the patient loses confidence and the warm feeling towards the therapist turn cold.

The term the "Stockholm syndrome" was coined by my police colleague Dr. Harvey Schlossberg, a police detective who became a clinical psychologist. It refers to an incident which took place in Stockholm, Sweden. A person entered the Stockholm Credit Bank and attempted an armed robbery. The confrontation with responding police officers prompted the robber to take three women and a man hostage. He retreated into the open bank vault with his victims and demanded that the police bring to the scene, from prison, a former associate. Together, he and his cohort held off the authorities for six days.

At the end of those six days the perpetrators finally surrendered. On exiting the vault, the hostages used their bodies to protect the captors from any possible police bullets. They had formed a ring around their captors, and begged that the police not shoot. Later, while being interviewed by the media, one of the young female victims expressed very warm feelings about one of the captors. It was reported that she would wait until he was released from jail and that she might even marry him. Many people were shocked at hearing this and even conjectured that something sexual must have occurred between the two of them during the long incarceration in the vault. But in actuality no sexual liaison had occurred. The perpetrator had on a few occasions even placed a gun barrel under the chin of the hostage, and paraded her for the authorities to see. It was also reported that they had wired the hostages by their necks to the drawers of the safe deposit boxes when they thought the police were going to throw in tear gas. The hostage-takers said they thought that the gas would cause their captives to pass out and strangle themselves, but that it would be the fault of the authorities and not theirs. In spite of these actions, the female hostage's emotional feelings remained the same, inexplicable even to herself.

This phenomenon has been repeated many times, all over the world in countless incidents. After many interviews with former hostages, there seems to be one group less likely to be subject to this reaction. Long-term career diplomats, and with no slight intended, especially British diplomatic types, seem less vulnerable to this emotional transference. Sir Geoffrey Jackson, who was held captive for 168 days by the Tupamaros in Uruguay, managed to wear out his captors and "almost get control of them." American career diplomat Moorhead Kennedy, held in Iran for 444 days, also evidenced a lack of this emotional relationship with his captors.

One of the new problems that we in negotiating and hostage recovery are seeing is an adamant denial by recently released hostages that they had experienced this syndrome with their captors. It is especially difficult for airline flight crews or other "in-charge" persons to accept that they may have experienced these emotional ties with their captors. To admit to this would cause them to feel they had "lost control" of themselves in this situation.

The media in some instances has mistakenly equated the Stockholm syndrome with brainwashing of the *Manchurian Candidate* type. This is most definitely not true. Transference or the Stockholm syndrome is a coping mechanism that may very well help one to survive. Authorities actually encourage it, since it is less likely the perpetrator will harm his victim if he has developed any relationship with him. This relationship will develop between hostage and captor mutually, and also between perpetrator and negotiator in a confined hostage situation. It does not usually develop between the hostage and the negotiator, because the hostage regards the authorities as the reason they are being held. More than one victim believes that "if only they would give him what he wants, then we would be freed."

Can there then be such a thing as a negative transference? The answer is yes. Homicide is often the extreme culmination of such a negative relationship. Fortunately this is a *very rare* occurrence and not likely to happen. There was an incident in Frankfurt, Germany, when after 17 hours the perpetrator fell asleep. The hostage then relieved his captor of his gun and shot him in the head.

A simple illustration of positive transference, should you still question its value, would be to observe first-

time airline passengers. They will talk incessantly to anyone near them. They will relate the most intimate details
of their life, all the while gripping the armrests with
white knuckles. While flying, they are in crisis. They
must share that crisis with another human being—any
human being available. The same applies to a hostage
situation or hijacking. It is a crisis for all involved. Once
the nervous passenger is on the ground, or the hostages
are released, the crisis passes and the person returns to
his normal behavior and inhibitions.

Remember this about transference: you will not experience a mental breakdown or become a "traitor" if you
get along with your captors. It is what will keep you
alive. There are skilled mental health professionals who
can deal with the aftermath of victimization, but if you
are dead there is no one who can help you.

Violence, Death or Panic

Though violence and death are traumatic to the close observer during a hijacking or hostage situation, the authorities must deal with these tragedies in an objective, seemingly callous manner. An assessment must be made. Was this the result of a panic, a "fight or flight" reaction, or of a deranged mind.

In the preparation of our hostage negotiation techniques in 1972, we believed that even if someone were killed or seriously injured during the original action (prior to the establishment of dialogue with the perpetrator), we would still probably be able to establish contact with that subject and utilize negotiating techniques to effect the safe release of the remaining hostages. Studies indicate that the majority of police officers killed in the line of duty meet their deaths during the first few seconds of an unexpected confrontation. The suspect is in a panic reaction and during this "fight or flight" stage he strikes out at that which is causing his panic. Next he looks about to try and find a way to flee from the source of this panic.

We have trained law enforcement officers to take that step back, to "take cover" and to allow the panic to subside so that the perpetrator may return to a more rational appraisal of his situation.

You as a hostage, if caught up in this situation, must play it extremely cool. Any quick, sudden or unexpected actions—any imprudent resistance on your part—may direct the panic reaction toward you, with subsequent pain and suffering. Follow his instructions and keep a low profile.

In many terrorist hijackings, carried out by a limited number of perpetrators, the initial takeover was accompanied by a lot of noise, bravado and often violence and bloodshed. This was in order to establish fear in a large number of people. Even if the wounds were for the most part superficial, a little bright red blood for "show" from a bloodied nose is usually enough for people to take notice of what is happening. Once again, avoiding the aisle or front row seats might spare you from that kind of fate.

In some instances persons have contributed to their

own injury or demise by their unwitting actions. Some attempted to overpower their captors but were unsuccessful, or did not receive help from fellow captives. The perpetrator may deal harshly with such persons, or may even kill them in "self-defense," notwithstanding that he started the episode in the first place.

In other situations, as we saw on the Kuwaiti Airline hijacking in 1985, and TWA Flight 847, just being an American or an Israeli has made some passengers targets of their captors. These actions, as well as others such as killing hostages on "deadlines," will be further evidence of the deranged minds of the hostage-takers. Barring any intelligence gathered to the contrary, these actions will usually bring about a rescue attempt by the authorities. It is realized from past experience that rescue attempts can be hazardous both to the hostages as well as to the rescuers. One need only to look back in 1971 to Attica, a prison in N.Y. State. Ten hostages were killed by gunfire during their "rescue." Their inmate captors had no firearms.

In 1985 an Egyptian commando team attempted a rescue in Malta. Here 58 were reportedly killed, many by gunshot, after a fire started from the rescuers' flash grenades. The authorities in these cases, as in others, could not just stand by and watch as the perpetrators rolled body after body out as deadlines passed. Sometimes the risks must be taken and can be done successfully, especially if the rescuers are well-trained and well-equipped.

Avoiding the Problem

Medical professionals and insurance companies have long since postulated that an "ounce of prevention is worth a pound of cure." Nowhere could that axiom be more appropriate than in this field of self-protection. If you are never taken, then you will not need to cope with being a hostage.

The term "hardening the target" means to make you or your group less desirable to these wrong-doers. It may sound very unChristian to say "let the perpetrators go on to someone else," but if they are frustrated by many "hardened targets" it is possible they will give up their particular act of violence entirely. It is more likely, though, that they will opt for safer and "softer" targets.

A classic example of the effects of hardening a target is the case of Sir Geoffrey Jackson, the British ambassador to Uruguay. While he was eventually kidnapped, it required an increase in his abductors from 6 to almost 25. Sir Geoffrey had noted a great deal of surveillance at his diplomatic office. He had notified the British Home Office, and he had even considered closing his diplomatic offices. They had advised him to take greater precautions to protect himself. This he did, changing routines as well as vehicles and travel routes. Each of these steps, he later learned while incarcerated, added to the difficulty of his abduction. He learned it required the perpetrators to increase surveillance, use more manpower and eventually increase their planning. His captors had wanted Sir Geoffrey as an important hostage, and they were able to increase the number of people needed to get him. (In some cases this may not be an option of the perpetrators.) After several months of holding Sir Geoffrey, his captors were unable to accomplish their underlying goals. This was due to a great degree to Sir Geoffrey's own conduct, demeanor and personal preparation.

Other preventive measures are simple enough that they might well become part of your everyday routine. These would include such measures as looking through the window or door of a bank or store before entering. If you see people with their hands over their heads, or a person with a gun, don't go in. Many people have blundered their way into the midst of an armed robbery or other terrorist act simply by not paying attention. I've often heard people in some parts of the country say they don't have a key to their front doors because they don't have a lock on it. Well, in some places that may still be the case, but they are becoming few and far between. Without becoming paranoid, you can take some simple precautions to increase your general safety. Lock your door. Use a peep-hole or window to identify unexpected callers. By doing this you may avoid becoming a victim.

There was an instance when a bank vice-president and his family were home watching TV. There was a knock at the door, and his teen-age son opened it without looking or inquiring. Three masked men pushed their way in and kidnapped the banker, his wife and their children. Everyone was tied up and held overnight until the father was taken to his bank in the morning in an effort to rob the vault. After many hours of explaining, the banker was able to convince the would-be robbers that he would be unable to bypass the "time-lock" procedures and open the vault. The criminals aborted their robbery attempt and no one was physically hurt.

The entire episode could easily have been avoided if the teenage boy either inquired who was at the door or had looked through a window or peephole before unlocking the door. The perpetrators would easily have been recognized as dangerous and not admitted.

As we have seen, the banking industry remains a prized target for criminals looking to "make a score." Also in these times of turmoil, those individuals involved in "domestic terrorism" have targeted bank executives as well as high-ranking corporate personnel and their families as a source of revenue to finance their disruptive acts against society.

And finally, for everyone, avoidance is the best procedure to follow to insure unmolested survival. AWARENESS!! BE ALERT!!

1. AT HOME: Follow basic security procedures. Lock, look, and listen.
2. SHOPPING: Look into the store before entering. Pay attention to what is going on around you.
3. WORK: When going to and coming from, avoid routine, take different routes, be aware of strangers.
4. WORKPLACE: Don't have direct access to your office. Have secretary, receptionist, partitions, a locked rear exit.
5. TRAVEL: Make no announcement of travel plans, fly U.S. carriers or secure foreign airlines.
6. HOTELS: Have patience and spend the dollar to have the bellman escort you to your room, especially in an unfamiliar hotel.

Kidnappings vs. Hostage Situations

In a *hostage situation*, the victim is held against his or her will by a perpetrator who is engaged in a confrontation with the authorities. The hostage is usually not taken for any intrinsic value, but rather for his value in gathering or influencing an audience, or for use as leverage against the authorities. Any demand for money in connection with the event is usually an afterthought. The hostage-taker uses the captive to get what he wants, be it escape, acknowledgment of a cause, or, as in a prison situation, a change in environment or procedures.

The key is the confrontation. The perpetrator, though

he may be unknown at the onset, will become recognizable to the victims, witnesses and authorities as the event unravels. Most hostage situations are not designed to kill, but to benefit the captor. Most often it has been during the "rescue" attempt that innocent lives have been lost, as in Attica in 1971 and Malta in 1985.

On the other hand, *kidnapping* is a crime where there is little or no confrontation. In this type of incident, the perpetrator has anonymity and mobility. The only person who might be able to identify him is the victim. The perpetrator, in order to ensure there will be no eyewitness, many times will do away with the captive. They may go so far as to dig a deep hole in a remote location, provide airpipes and possibly one or two days' supply of food and water. In this manner they can produce the captive if they need proof of his detention, or to prove he is still alive. If they should succeed or fail in obtaining the ransom, they may disclose the victim's location. They may also take off to parts unknown, leaving the victim to die.

In this type of kidnap situation it is advised that the victim make a point of indicating that he does not even want to look at his captors, so that he would be unable to identify or even describe them. Assuring the perpetrator the anonymity that he needs, may well assure your safety.

Organized kidnap teams, such as we have seen in Italy, Sardinia or in Central and South America, often finance their political causes by using ransoms collected in this "specialty crime." Because they will often rely on "repeat business," they require a degree of credibility. When the payment is received, they will return the victim. In this manner, they build a reputation that payment will bring about the safe release of a loved one. This makes it seem that they can be "trusted," and it will make any future jobs that much easier for them. Care must be taken in negotiating these types of cases. In one instance, a security organization attempted to reduce the size of the ransom demanded. They assumed the hardline position that only one-half of the ransom could be raised. The perpetrators then replied that they would send back half of the victim, and "which half did they want?"

The ransom, "to pay or not to pay," is a decision that should be made by the families or corporations involved. In the case of international kidnappings, it is the stated policy of the U.S. government not to pay any ransom to anyone. Yet there have been instances where unofficially much logistical assistance has been rendered by our government.

In domestic kidnapping, do not look to the local police to advise you one way or the other about ransom payments. That decision is yours, and is usually based on the financial means of the family or corporations involved. Most police and FBI representatives will assist in the acquiring, wrapping and even the delivery of the ransom, if so requested. It is the policy of every law enforcement agency in the U.S. that I have had contact with that "THE LIFE OF THE VICTIM IS PARAMOUNT." Criminals can be captured later, the money can probably be recovered, but, above all, life is sacred.

A note to families. . . . Invariably, you will be informed by the perpetrators not to contact the police, "if you ever wish to see your loved ones again." There is no guarantee that they do not intend to hurt the victim, no matter how closely you follow their instructions. As a matter of fact, in most instances where the police were not notified, some harm has come to the victim. One suggestion to minimize the possibility of the kidnappers' knowing if the police are called, is to call the local "Chief of Detectives" or FBI office, and advise them of the facts known, as well as the warning against police intervention. Most agencies have a "civilian clothes" response team, just in case the perpetrators have your residence under surveillance.

Another suggestion if the notification was made by telephone is to: 1) Note as close as possible the exact time the call came in. Some telephone systems can identify incoming calls. 2) Request to speak to the victim to insure it is not a hoax. 3) Try to write down as much information about the call as possible, especially a) exact conversation as close to verbatim as you can b) the person or persons' voice—tone, pitch, accents, c) any background noises, i.e. cars, trains, airplane, bells, whatever.

All of this information, as insignificant as it may seem, will assist the authorities in trying to rescue the victim.

If you are in a business where the likelihood of your being kidnapped exists, pre-condition yourself and your family. Being alert and aware will many times prevent the unfortunate from happening. Most kidnappers will select the easier target, so send him on his way.

Many corporate executives, upon taking high-risk positions, will wisely take the time to prepare a "personal" profile folder. It consists of biographies, photos, phone numbers, medical histories and any other pertinent information that might assist the authorities in verifying a reported kidnapping. This pre-incident planning should not be limited to executives and businessmen. One need only look at the backs of milk cartons at breakfast to see one or two missing children, and you see it could happen anywhere. The ordinary citizen should not live in fear, but a few simple precautions may help avoid any pain associated with the kidnapping or abduction of a loved one. No one thinks it will happen to them, but sometimes people are mistaken for other people, or you may be valuable to a kidnapper for some reason you cannot imagine.

I can't stress it enough, KEEP YOUR DOORS LOCKED. In your home it may be inconvenient to stop what you are doing to let the kids in. There are still folks who tell me they don't even have a key because they never lock their doors. Well, times have changed. Police departments are bigger, most prisons are overcrowded by Federal court standards and no area is immune to conflict. From the farm lands in our country with their economic problems, to the Northern and Western cities with their drug-related crime, to the Southern cities with the influx of new immigrants and refugees, all can be the source of hostage or kidnap incidents.

Keeping your car doors locked as well, may prevent any uninvited guests or passengers who may very well rob or attack you. Women who keep their pocketbooks on the passenger seat with the windows rolled down may be inviting a theft at the next traffic light. Men who drive with their arm out the window, holding on to the door frame in heavy traffic may lose their wristwatch to a fleet-footed robber who can run against traffic in his "felony shoes" (athletic footwear). Leaving your car door locked when parked may prevent someone from popping up unexpectedly from your backseat.

Victimology

When the hostage becomes a former hostage, he or she also has now become a victim. There will be a great period of readjustment. Some former hostages will want to talk over the past events, to bring the incident into perspective. Others may become reticent, and prefer not to talk or even think about what they have been through. Both of these types of individuals need to be helped through the experience.

The diagram on the next page displays in visual terms the premise that in any hostage/kidnapping or terrorist incident there are more victims than the obvious hostages. Though I do not wish to demean the crisis experienced by the primary victim, we shall try to cover the problems for and effects on all the "victims" of the incident.

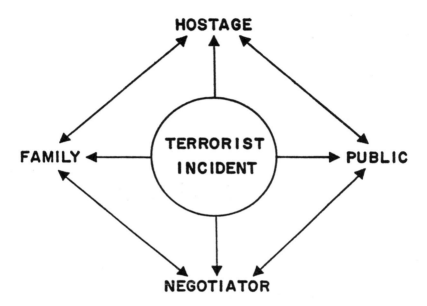

Short Term

Most criminal, emotional or prison incidents are short-term hostage situations. The hostage is intended to be used as a lever against the authorities. The goal may be a quick and safe escape or to bring immediate attention to a grievance. These incidents will usually occur in places of business, residences and public areas such as airports, buses, banks and building lobbies.

As indicated in an earlier chapter, the first few moments are the most dangerous. The initial panic reaction can cause people to get hurt. Follow orders explicitly, especially in these first crucial moments. It is reported that in the Beverly Hills incident at Van Cleef and Arpels, the security officer was told by the perpetrator to keep quiet. The officer continued to talk and was almost immediately stabbed by the would-be robber. Remember to follow orders quickly and without hesitation. After the situation has calmed down there will be time enough to encourage transference, or the Stockholm syndrome.

Remember also during any incarceration, but especially in fast-moving, short-term incidents, that negotiators should never close off the problem-solving dynamics for the perpetrator. One almost certain way to lead a perpetrator from frustration to aggression is to tell him "NO!" This will require him to demonstrate that he still has his power, and he may do that by harming a hostage, especially the messenger who brings the "bad news." They are the most immediate and vulnerable target. In the case in Beverly Hills, when the hostage-messenger told the perpetrator that the police would not let a television crew inside the store, he killed the messenger. This demonstrated his displeasure and seriousness for the authorities.

The principal victim, the hostage, is the most visible to the observer. He or she will experience the most immediate effects of the incident. The first realization that something is awry, may bring about an emphatic denial. "No this can't be happening to me. This happens to other people, you read about it in the papers. Not me, not my family!" There may be paralyzing fear and a panic reaction. Physiologically the automatic nervous system will respond by dumping adrenalin into the blood stream. Your pulse will race, your hair will stand on end, you will breakout in goosebumps and your muscles will tense. You may tend to almost hyperventilate. On the other hand, some people might exhibit an opposite response. Blood may rush to their stomach and they will get dizzy or pass out.

After acceptance of the situation, people will respond in many different ways. Some begin to tremble uncontrollably or break out in a cold sweat. Others will seemingly show no reaction, staring in a catatonic state. An individual may lose bladder or bowel control. Many will experience a strong guilt reaction; "If only I had not done this, gone here, etc."

Another interesting response comes from those persons who outwardly appear to be at a "Roman holiday"; this is an almost festive response, "making the best of a bad situation." In one incident a young single guy (who was probably lonely) enjoyed his new-found notoriety while a gunman held him and several others hostage in a bank. During the course of negotiations, some sandwiches and a six-pack of beer were sent into the bank. This hostage reportedly ate three sandwiches and drank three cans of beer. Later he convinced the perpetrator to send out for two more six-packs. Even after the ordeal, which had lasted nine hours, and the lengthy interview by the assistant district attorney, this victim requested to join the police who were having a "debriefing" at a nearby restaurant. When later questioned, he said that he wanted to "keep the party going."

He, of course, was an extreme exception to the reaction of other people involved in the same incident. One of the other hostages, a female bank teller, stated that a few days after her release she noticed her hair falling out in clumps. Another young lady was unable to ride the subway, since this was the manner she normally travelled to her job in the bank. She could not cope with the anxiety created by this simple action.

The manager of this bank and the one at another bank incident handled their separate crises by acting as the "captain of the ship," concerning themselves with the safety of their employees. This was evident when, after having been covertly spirited out of the bank, the second manager insisted on returning inside to "care for his employees." However, when later interviewed, the second manager reported long-term insomnia, and when sleep did come he was troubled by nightmares.

The first bank manager had appeared on numerous TV interviews after the incident. He indicated that talking about the ordeal had helped to lessen his inability to sleep and had helped in coping. When later anxiety attacks prompted him to request time off from work, he was met with statements such as, "He's trying to milk this forever." In the final analysis this manager quit the banking business and began pursuing another career. His price was his education (an MBA in banking), training, seminars, and years of hard work—all down the drain.

In another incident, again involving a banker, his home was invaded by three thugs who wanted him to open a bank vault. The criminals gained access when the banker's teenaged son unwittingly answered the door without looking to see who was there. After this 7-hour ordeal, where the wife, son and daughter were bound and gagged, the psychological toll was:

   a) The banker left his financial career.
   b) The son required extensive psychiatric care to cope with the guilt he felt for jeopardizing his family.
   c) The wife continued to experience uncontrollable fits of crying.

One of the hostages held when the B'nai B'rith building was taken over by a Hanafi Muslim sect in Washington, D.C., in 1976, did manage to cope successfully in the aftermath. When awakened from sleep by nightmares, he would sit down and write out all that he could remember about the incident. After a short while, this journal had helped him to cope with the experience, and he was able to get back to sleep. This catharsis, either verbal or written, can help the victim put the ordeal behind him.

Many of the symptoms and traumatic scars of even a short-term hostage incident can last a very long time. After 10 years, the young victims of the hijacking of a schoolbus in Chowchilla, California, which was subsequently buried with them inside until they were rescued, still have problems. Some are reportedly still under psychiatric care.

Children

This brings us to the special problem facing the young. A hostage incident is difficult for anyone, but its effects may be more lasting and devastating to children. The tragedy at a McDonald's restaurant in San Ysidro, California, where a disturbed gunman in military camouflage clothing wounded and killed many adults and children, left many psychological scars in the young people. Seeing the murders, and then seeing the response of Police SWAT teams also dressed in camouflage, did much to heighten the anxiety of the children. This "warfare" left many tearful and frightened children, with lasting psychological trauma. Thoughtfully, rather than leave the restaurant as a constant reminder, the McDonald's corporation razed the building.

The Moluccan terrorist takeover of one hundred schoolchildren in 1978, as well as other similar terrorist incidents in the Netherlands, brought about reported mandatory psychiatric care for all former hostages. Here in the United States, a school with 150 children in Cokesville, Wyoming, was taken over by two fanatics in 1986. The incident ended when one of the bombs the pair had brought in exploded. David Young and his wife had attempted to extort $300 million dollars from the federal government, at the rate of $2 million per hostage. The bomb exploded when Young handed it to his wife. She apparently detonated the device accidently in front of the children, injuring 74 of them and killing herself. David Young then committed suicide. This tragic incident brought a flood of volunteer mental health professionals who continue to assist in the rehabilitation and readjustment of these young victims. The main thrust of the treatment in Wyoming seems to have been confrontational or reality therapy. The taking of the children back to the school and having them talk about what had happened, the facing of the incident and its aftermath, have helped the victims cope with the experience. This kind of approach should only be taken with the support of mental health professionals.

Long-term

Most long-term incidents are usually kidnap situations, where the victim is stalked for a period of time and then taken and held in a usually well-organized operation. After the usual stage of denial ("Why me?") similar to the short-term victim's, the long-term incident will take on a different complexion for the victim.

Usually these terrorist incidents are undertaken by an organized group, but that does not mean they are "professional" in their actions. They may be highstrung, tense and easily shaken. Sudden movements should be avoided, as mentioned in a previous chapter. These actions may be interpreted by the captors as an escape attempt or assault, prompting them to defend themselves.

Usually the captors will be carrying weapons, which they may or may not know how to use. You cannot assume you are being held by a professional terrorist organization. They are usually random groups of people, at best ranging from intelligence officers to mentally deranged thugs picked up for the occasion. When you are taken, they will try to break you by threats, beatings or fear of death. Be prepared to accept this fact, and don't challenge them.

Isolated confinement has other harsh effects, especially if it is in a windowless environment. The inability to distinguish day and night, the removal of your watch—these factors can serve to disorient you. This is especially true when you awake from your first sleep in captivity. In this seclusion you may feel you are losing touch with reality. Try to keep a calendar of some sort, using your own sleep habits, those of your captors, or the routines that emerge as a guide. Outside sounds can suggest the time of day, such as a rooster crowing, church bells or even traffic. Establish routines for yourself, both physically as well as mentally. After you have "settled in," try not to dwell on the discomforts or fears you might be experiencing. Remember, if your captors had intended to kill you, you would already be dead. In most cases you are worth more alive to them than dead. Be cautious and you will probably make it out alive.

When finally released, there will be many things for you to cope with. In addition to the insomnia, possible nightmares and other bodily disruptions, there are other things you will have to face. Victims whose wives had given birth, or had infants growing up during the time of their incarceration, have additional feelings to deal with. The former hostage may feel awkward when a child doesn't recognize him, or cowers in fear at the "stranger in the house." Though ecstatic with his freedom, the victim may feel "cheated" out of several once-in-a-lifetime milestones: Christenings, baby's first step, Bar Mitzvah, graduation, weddings. Holidays that have passed can often times be made up. Many families have left the Christmas tree up and decorated with presents waiting for the hostage's homecoming. This caring can make the return home to loved ones even sweeter for the victim.

Some of the other psychological reactions to captivity may include being startled easily, shame for having been captured in the first place and not making good an escape, and various guilt reactions. Victims may feel guilty for the sacrifices others had made on their behalf. There may have been others taken hostage as a result of their capture. Victims may experience decreased motivation, change in or an erratic temperament, and other phobic reactions. Physically they may have loss of appetite, unexplainable episodes of dizziness, or sexual dysfunctions. There may be the phenomenon of a "near-death experience" and its aftermath.

All of these reactions, both physical and psychological, are completely normal, and will usually fade with time.

For most people, it is advantageous to return to their normal lifestyle, work, school or profession as soon as possible. Those who seem to have the most difficult times are those who have not been kept busy. Of the 52 hostages who were released after 444 days of captivity in the U.S. embassy in Iran, the Marines, who left the Corps because their enlistments were up, had more difficulty readjusting than the civilians who returned to work. Barry Rosen, one of these 52 American hostages, reports in his book that the month-long whirlwind homecoming for the hostages helped make their adjustment easier and quicker. It helped remove much of the guilt or self-criticism that many hostages in different circumstances feel when they return home with much less fanfare. In this situation these men and women represented America held hostage—hostage to Iran as well as to the media. America and Americans needed a morale boost, and the victory of their release and the subsequent celebrations did just that. In this situation the hostages and the public helped each other.

In addition to this public support, the four days spent at the U.S. Air Force Hospital in Weisbaden, Germany (a place that would be used a few more times for later hostages), gave the released hostages the benefit of medical and psychiatric examination and care without the undeserved stigma sometimes given to persons who seek assistance from mental health professionals.

These previously stated reactions are the more obvious results of captivity. Physical survival is paramount. The emotional scars and trauma can be treated, shame and humiliation can quickly fade with support. If you are a corpse because you "tried to make a point," there is little that can be done for you except a fancy funeral. If you remember that the key is *survival*, you can and will make it.

Family

The victim of the hostage or terrorist incident is the one most often highlighted. But this incident also indelibly affects the lives of the victim's family and loved ones.

During an ongoing hostage situation, it will often seem that the police ignore the needs and concerns of the families involved. Because of this, and the ongoing crisis and confusion, the family will become the object of misinformation and rumor. Often the first notification of the incident will come from a "special report" or "news bulletin" on radio or television. This is often followed by a deluge of phone calls and inquiries by the media. It is difficult many times to confirm or give reaction to an incident you may have only just heard about. It is difficult to react to something that will indirectly affect your life.

The families may also experience the sleepless nights and nightmares, especially if they witness the event "live" on television or proceed to the scene of the incident. As indicated earlier, the presence of family members at the scene does not insure that they will be better informed. As a matter of fact, the turmoil, guns and action may add to the anxiety of the experience.

In a kidnapping, the family faces the first impact alone. If the kidnapping takes place in the home and the family is present, they become witnesses to the act, its terror and violence. If the victim is taken outside of the home and the notification comes from a visit by the FBI or a local police detective, then the family can only imagine what took place. Many times one's imagination can summon up a more devastating scene than the actual incident.

The first few days of a kidnapping are very stressful, even with the support of relatives and friends. The police and authorities set up the investigation, the ever-present media and their thirst for information keep the mind occupied. But as time passes the crowd disperses, support appears to diminish and depression sets in. As time passes, more and more strength is required merely to exist. Other less spectacular needs crop up . . . groceries to be bought, the mortgage, the car that won't start, a birthday or anniversary, and an empty lonely bed during sleepless nights.

As more time passes, it's the anniversary of the event

that becomes news: "How does it feel after a month, a year, etc." These are the times that require even more personal strength, in whatever manner you can muster it.

Probably the most devastating hostage crisis that would affect both primary victims and families took place in a diner in Westbury, N.Y., on Memorial Day, 1982. Four armed men invaded the diner and robbed the patrons. They then beat, raped and sodomized some of the customers, forcing the others to watch helplessly as their wives and companions were victimized. The men, who were unable to prevent the incident or protect their women, were also victimized and humiliated. This incident brought lasting psychological trauma to many of the persons involved.

Barbara Rosen, wife of Barry Rosen (one of the American Embassy hostages held in Iran), pointed up another problem facing families. She eventually became a media regular during the 444 days, joining other vocal hostage families in a sort of celebrity status. In the first few weeks of incarceration of her husband and the other 51 hostages, she felt there would be strength in anonymity and numbers. She felt that the individuality of the hostages should not be stressed, although the media felt quite the opposite. The media hounded the more "photogenic" families.

On her first network interview, Barbara used the term "terrorist" to describe the militia holding the embassy. Later realizing how it sounded, she asked for that word to be deleted from the tape. The producer said it couldn't be done, though other editing was done to enhance the newsman's "star" appearance. Also when she asked for a copy of the videotape interview to show Barry on his return, she was told (with no sign of embarrassment) that it would cost her $150. After more than a year of being a celebrity, Barbara had learned how to deal with the media. As she was leaving on her way to the long-awaited reunion with Barry, a reporter asked her what her first words would be to her husband. She replied, "Don't you think he should be the first one to hear that?"

She had waited in the U.S. for Barry to return, unlike some of the families who had felt an immediate need to be with the ex-hostages. Barbara Rosen felt that Barry needed this time to get well, both physically and mentally, before she considered her own needs and desires.

As far as children are concerned, their awareness is sometimes very simple. After a long separation and the subsequent homecoming, any further separation such as a short business trip will become time for worry. "Will Daddy be coming home again, or will he be staying away?" These statements and the accompanying anxiety will indicate that even the children in the family do experience psychological trauma.

Families, in general, have greater difficulty in readjustment than the hostages. As of 1982, in the U.S. Embassy hostage families there were four divorces and three separations of 26 married hostages. Many of the problems are with the wives of the hostages who no longer have the "independence and center-stage recognition." During their husbands' captivity, they became used to making decisions for themselves; when their husbands were released they found it difficult to return to the lifestyle that had prevailed previous to the incident. A similar phenomenon was seen in the return of the POW's and MIA's after the Vietnam War. Families had survived during their absence, bills had been paid and things had approached "normal" to some degree in the families. But at the time of the "homecoming" a few things became different. It is now assumed that the roles will return to "normal" and the returning spouse will take charge and make the decisions. The male hostages pick-up where they left off, most returning to a career and a future.

The Public

The price the public pays for hostage and terrorist incidents must be measured in various ways. The first is in psychological costs.

The summer of 1986 will live in the memories of travel agents, not as a banner year for business, but as the year when many people changed their plans for travel abroad to "see America first." This apparently came about after the hijacking of the cruise ship *Achille Lauro*, the explosion and deaths aboard Flight 840, and the massacres at the Rome and Vienna airports, where women and children were also indiscriminately killed.

People cancelled trips to the Mediterranean, the Middle East and to Europe as well. Notably the countries that suffered the greatest economic losses due to "terrorist actions" were NATO or pro-American countries. The vacationing public opted for travel in the U.S., Hawaii or the Caribbean.

One business that has seen an almost meteoric rise in terms of money spent has been that of security. Once considered a non-revenue-producing drain on the corporate structure, security has now become an integral part of the overall operation. The cost of these programs have, with little or no exception, been passed onto the public in higher costs.

For example, one large oil company previously a victim of kidnapping/terrorism in Latin America has the following security procedure: When a non-employee enters from any of three sides of the building, he is funneled to a large security desk complex, which is also under video-surveillance. Anywhere from four to six persons are behind the counter, where you are asked to state your business, who you are to see, whether or not you are expected, and to produce some identification. You are then registered, receive a temporary I.D. pass which is then affixed to your person, and are requested to open briefcases or packages for inspection. The security clerk telephones the office of the person you are to visit. His secretary or another office worker must stop what they are doing, report to the security desk and escort you to your destination.

When totalled, the cost of employee hours spent on security is extremely high, as is the cost of staff specifically assigned to security. Yet when placed against the possibility of a $14-million-dollar kidnapping, or the disruption of world-wide computer operations (one corporation has figured their "down time" as worth between $4 and $5 million dollars an hour), the expense of security is part of "the cost of doing business."

In 1986 the losses in the tourism and travel industry were astronomical. Cruise ship lines in the Mediterranean were unable to book sufficient passengers to operate at even a reasonable loss, so they cancelled many cruises entirely. Airlines, because of schedule regulations, were required to operate flights anyway—at tremendous financial loss. Some airlines flew almost empty aircraft or engaged in giveaway programs at a cost of hundreds of thousands of dollars. One airline even gave away a Rolls-Royce to encourage travel. These costs by necessity were passed onto the stockholders and eventually to the flying public.

In the summer of 1986, Pan American World Airways instituted a $5 security charge on its international flights to cover the cost of additional personnel and equipment to screen and search passengers and luggage. Some may recall that in the early 1970's, due to "skyjackings," a $3 airport tax was levied to cover the basic airport security which we have come to take for granted.

Another example of the long-term consequences of terrorism is what has reportedly happened to the motion picture industry in Ireland. There had been a number of bombings in theaters, and these were then followed by numerous threats. Each of these bomb-scares required evacuation and interruption of the film showings. Eventually, after the numerous threats and the occasional real device, they cut so deeply into the viewing public's attendance that most of the theaters were closed. It caused the loss of jobs in this and other related fields, and the virtual disappearance of an industry.

The Negotiator

In every hostage or kidnap incident the person against whom the act of violence is committed or who is held captive is easily recognized as the victim of the incident. Few if any observers remark on the other victims of these episodes. I would like to consider another of the "victims" of the hostage-taking or kidnapping: the police or law-enforcement agency. Let us focus specifically on the negotiator.

At the report of the incident the negotiator will have to respond. This will require him to stop whatever he is doing and travel immediately to the scene to commence the rescue attempt. If at work, he will drop whatever he is doing or pass it off to a colleague. If off-duty, he may well leave his wife and family at home or a friend's house, or in a shopping mall, and then proceed to "the job."

The family of the negotiator will also pay part of the price. The author's wife once said that while watching a live TV report showing the actual negotiations at a bank with an armed assailant, an interesting thought occurred. If I were shot and killed, she would not need to wait for the police chaplain to arrive to "break the news," she would have seen it live, in living color. These stresses plus the middle-of-the-night phone calls and responses add to the overall price paid by the negotiator and his family.

In long-term situations such as kidnappings or extended hostage situations the negotiator's private life is affected even more. The social functions cancelled, the spouse and family plans that must be readjusted, and the threat of physical danger that can possibly affect their own, seemingly removed family, all take their toll.

Post Incident

When the incident ends, the hostages are released and united with their loved ones. The perpetrator is handcuffed and led away into police custody, and the glow of TV lights silhouette the interviewers as you are trying to catch your breath. The negotiator may take two or three glasses of water, and walk around a bit to get his bearings. Under the glare of TV lights, a dozen or so strangers are all asking different questions about the incident at the same time. The negotiator has just gone through three to ten hours of tension, panic, stress, sorrow and terror. Finally, he experiences the release of all those pressures almost as though it were a physical orgasm. He is congratulated by all around, and then packs up his gear and heads for home.

It is at this point, when he is all alone, that the stress and pressures catch up with the negotiator. Early on in this new discipline, we learned that many of our officers were going through various multi-dimensional experiences. These were manifested by various physiological as well as psychological problems. They ranged from insomnia, loss of appetite and stomach problems to sexual dysfunction and even heart attacks. This, even though the negotiators had undergone cardiovascular examinations prior to assuming their roles. One negotiator, while driving home after an incident, had to pull his car over on the side of the road. He was crying uncontrollably and could not see to drive because of the tears. I experienced many of these symptoms early in my career. It has been my experience in dealing with negotiators across the country and overseas, that many if not all had experienced these symptoms but felt awkward expressing them.

A few years into the program, by chance observation I realized that many of the previously described symptoms were not always evident if the incident ended at an early hour. When the team retired to a bar or restaurant and spent two or three hours "talking out the job," a good deal of the stress was shed. Many negotiators drank only soft drinks or milk, so alcohol is not essential to the process.

In speaking with my colleague Dr. Harvey Schlossberg about this, we realized that what we were doing was engaging in "group therapy sessions." This should not take on any negative connotations, for in fact it was a type of "stress management."

Another reality is the euphoric high that the principal or primary negotiator will experience. After many appearances and TV interviews, he has a sort of celebrity status. This will usually last anywhere from a day to a week, and will be followed by a vacant feeling as this recognition starts to fade. It is not uncommon for the negotiator to go into a mild depression. The analogy to a fighter-pilot has been made: "Hours of boredom interrupted by moments of sheer terror."

The negotiator will be looking and waiting for the next job, to bathe in the limelight once again. This sometimes creates additional difficulties for the officer in his normal duties. It is not uncommon for one to experience overt as well as covert jealousies within the law enforcement agency, from supervisors as well as from peer officers.

Finally, remember that these feelings are real, and though unique are not abnormal or unexpected. The hostage negotiator is experiencing deep feelings and emotions. The mental health professional associated with the negotiating team affords easy access to assistance in dealing with these feelings, without giving the negotiator the sense that he is stigmatized by them.

These pressures and stresses are part of the price paid by law enforcement for the privilege and honor of being able to help the victims of a hostage crisis.

The Rescue

Should the situation reach a point where the authorities, either by virtue of opportunity or necessity, deem that a physical assault to rescue you should be mounted, be prepared to react appropriately.

There have been large-scale rescues made by Israeli commandos at the Entebbe Airport, the Federal Republic of Germany's GSG9 Special Border Police rescue of a Lufthansa jet at Mogadishu, and Egyptian commandos at Larnaca, Cyprus. There was also the large-scale operation at the Iranian mission at Princess Gate in London. And lest we forget, the ill-fated rescue attempt by U.S. Delta Forces at "Desert One" for the American hostages held in Iran. Most recently there has been the Egyptian commando rescue attempt at Malta, which left nearly sixty dead.

In each of these incidents there were casualties— among the hostages, the perpetrators and/or their rescuers. All of them were military operations, and accordingly had "acceptable casualty rates." From a civilian standpoint, hopefully you will not become an "acceptable casualty."

When might you expect a rescue attempt? There are various times and circumstances that are more likely to warrant an attempt. In the course of hostage negotiating, the deaths of hostages have been categorized in order to deal with the problems of hostage recovery. Persons who are killed or injured during the initial takeover are deemed victims of a "panic reaction." As tragic as these deaths are, authorities may still be able to negotiate in order to assure that no one else is injured. We have been able to do this even after a brother police officer was killed. On the other hand, if after dialogue has been established and a hostage is killed on a "deadline" for some inexplicable reason, this would indicate a deranged mind on the part of the hostage-taker. If he can kill one hostage, he can kill others. When faced with this situation, the authorities may opt to rescue the remaining hostages by force or deception, rather than wait for additional "executions." The gathering of intelligence at this point is critical.

Usually the rescue will be "announced" by a diversionary action. An explosion, a loud siren or noise, or a blinding flash. Should this happen, get down to protect yourself. Hit the deck with your hands covering your head and face; if in an aircraft assume the "crash position," leaning forward, head down. Listen for orders and follow them explicitly. Be prepared to possibly be manhandled and pushed around a bit. Remember that the rescuers will not know who is who, and they may need to treat you and everyone else as a possible perpetrator for their own safety as well as yours.

At Entebbe when the Israelis were making the rescue, it was reported that a hostage stood up to see what was happening, and was unfortunately shot by one of his would-be rescuers.

In training, police are taught that if deadly force must be used, that they must make accurate "target identification." After numerous incidents where hostages have been killed or injured because the perpetrators had changed clothing with them, the need for correct identification became very evident. An incident that vividly demonstrated this involved Attica, the prison in upstate New York, in 1971. Approximately 10 hostages were killed by gunfire during their "rescue." The inmates holding the hostages (who had changed clothes with their captives) had no firearms, so it must be assumed that the rescuing forces brought about their demise.

Another problem that rescue forces have been faced with is that when capture or capitulation is near the hostage-takers will attempt to create confusion. In some cases, they have caused the stampede of hostages, and have attempted to make good their own escape by "blending in with the crowd." One way the authorities have dealt with this type of problem is to place everyone, after a brief frisking for weapons, into a large bus. After transport to a secure facility or stationhouse, they are sorted and identified. Also at that time statements and evidence can be gathered, and the immediate as well as future needs of the former hostages can be identified. On one occasion, the identity of a perpetrator was easily made on the bus, because the hostages were beating their former captor. He, in turn, had to be rescued by the police.

Prosecution

One of the biggest problems that prosecutors and district attorneys have after the successful release of hostage or kidnap victims is the reluctance on the part of those released to assist in bringing their captors to justice. This is especially true if: a) The captivity was of a long duration, b) no one was physically injured, c) the perpetrator is handsome and/or has a cavalier personality and is well-spoken. These terms have been used by hostages to describe their captors.

If the incident is of a long duration, and the actual captors spend a great deal of time with the victims, various phenomena can occur. As we have discussed earlier, the Stockholm syndrome, psychological transference and survival identification are all modes of conduct by which persons in crises cope by relating to any other human beings that are physically close to them. This may occur even if the physical proximity is involuntary on the part of the victim. It may prevent animosities or anger from developing between the principals involved. Thus transference not only reinforces our desire to survive, but it provides a means.

This same lack of animosity has affected trained police officers who have negotiated for long periods of time with the perpetrators. It has not been uncommon for the negotiator to minimize the actions of the suspect with statements such as, "He didn't really mean to shoot at me, it must have been a warning shot," when in actuality it was not. This type of emotional attachment after many hours of negotiating can be dangerous to the safety of the officer negotiating, as well as potentially damaging to his or her psyche if deadly force might be required to apprehend the suspect. For this and other reasons, we do not have the negotiator act as the arresting officer.

No such relationship is likely to develop if the captors torture, beat or kill a victim. The 1985 Klinghoffer case on the Italian cruise ship *Achille Lauro* demonstrated this rather vividly. Leon Klinghoffer was a physically disabled man in his sixties. It is reported that one or two of the Palestinian terrorists who seized the ship shot him and dumped his body and wheelchair into the sea. His body washed ashore in Syria. It is also reported that when Mrs. Klinghoffer went to Italy to identify the terrorists for prosecution by the Italian courts, she spat in their faces. Other passengers from the ship also expressed a willingness to testify against the terrorists.

As heinous as the killing of a hostage is, there may still develop this type of transference relationship. The prolonged hijacking of a train by Moluccan extremists in Bellen Holland in 1976 demonstrated how strong this relationship could be in spite of several killings of captives. One of the captives who survived wrote letters to the family of one of the hijackers who had been killed. This went on for a number of years, and may still be going on.

In some kidnappings where the victim was particularly strong willed, he was able to resist the relationship with his captors by remaining strong and deviously dominant. This once again refers to the case of Sir Geoffrey Jackson kidnapped by the Tupamaros on January 8, 1971. His experiences are detailed in his book *Surviving the Long Night*.

It is extremely difficult for the district attorney or prosecutors to put together a proper case for court presentation in many of these situations. In one instance approximately 30 people were held hostage in a supermarket for five hours. Upon their release, some of the hostages were held for another seven hours by the assistant district attorney, while attempting to get statements for the court proceedings.

Your patience and assistance is very necessary to insure that the perpetrators do not "walk" on the indictment. In one instance in New Mexico a young man, James Andrew Johnson with the African name Gosundi Wusiya, held hostages to gain "jobs for the unemployed, homes for the homeless." These were surely honorable and laudable aims. After the hostages were released, a high-ranking member of the New Mexico State government declined prosecution. The perpetrator a few months later tried a similar action at the New York State offices at the World Trade Center. After the hostages were released and the perpetrator was taken into custody, he was given a preliminary psychiatric evaluation and then prosecuted. He did not get a "free ride" in New York.

Epilogue

Terrorism is a form of surrogate warfare conducted by nations or groups who, for whatever reasons, wish to bring about the downfall of western democracies. The victimization of innocent civilians to create that almost crippling atmosphere of fear is just a part of their arsenal.

Whether trying to create economic chaos by product tampering, sabotage, or disruption of the travel and vacation industries of our western allies, these groups threaten us all, and it is incumbent on all of us to do all we can to diminish their efforts. By taking some simple precautions, by being aware and alert we can add in great measure to our own safety and that of our families.

These precautions are by no means meant only for the

international traveler, diplomat or businessmen. Terrorism is defined in many ways, depending on the person experiencing it. A bank-teller facing the barrel of a gun in the sweaty hand of a nervous teenager is being terrorized. A supermarket clerk with a knife at her throat while the perpetrator shouts demands to the surrounding police, is being terrorized. The senior citizen robbed in the elevator, only to become a hostage when the police arrive, is also a victim of a "terrorist" incident.

We hope that these and the other incidents and examples we wrote about will heighten your awareness of how to protect yourself, and help you learn how to survive as a hostage.